ONE FOOT IN EDEN

by the same author

✱

COLLECTED POEMS, 1921–1951
THE VOYAGE AND OTHER POEMS
THE LABYRINTH
PROMETHEUS

EDWIN MUIR

One Foot in Eden

FABER AND FABER

24 Russell Square

London

First published in mcmlvi
by Faber and Faber Limited
24 Russell Square London W.C.1
Second impression mcmlvi
Printed in Great Britain by
R. MacLehose and Company Limited
The University Press Glasgow

To
WILLA

CONTENTS

I

11

II

I

MILTON

Milton, his face set fair for Paradise,
And knowing that he and Paradise were lost
In separate desolation, bravely crossed
Into his second night and paid his price.
There towards the end he to the dark tower came
Set square in the gate, a mass of blackened stone
Crowned with vermilion fiends like streamers blown
From a great funnel filled with roaring flame.

Shut in his darkness, these he could not see,
But heard the steely clamour known too well
On Saturday nights in every street in Hell.
Where, past the devilish din, could Paradise be?
A footstep more, and his unblinded eyes
Saw far and near the fields of Paradise.

THE ANIMALS

They do not live in the world,
Are not in time and space.
From birth to death hurled
No word do they have, not one
To plant a foot upon,
Were never in any place.

For with names the world was called
Out of the empty air,
With names was built and walled,
Line and circle and square,
Dust and emerald;
Snatched from deceiving death
By the articulate breath.

But these have never trod
Twice the familiar track,
Never never turned back
Into the memoried day.
All is new and near
In the unchanging Here
Of the fifth great day of God,
That shall remain the same,
Never shall pass away.

On the sixth day we came.

THE DAYS

Issuing from the Word
The seven days came,
Each in its own place,
Its own name.
And the first long days
A hard and rocky spring,
Inhuman burgeoning,
And nothing there for claw or hand,
Vast loneliness ere loneliness began,
Where the blank seasons in their journeying
Saw water at play with water and sand with sand.
The waters stirred
And from the doors were cast
Wild lights and shadows on the formless face
Of the flood of chaos, vast
Lengthening and dwindling image of earth and heaven.
The forest's green shadow
Softly over the water driven,
As if the earth's green wonder, endless meadow
Floated and sank within its own green light.
In water and night
Sudden appeared the lion's violent head,
Raging and burning in its watery cave.
The stallion's tread
Soundlessly fell on the flood, and the animals poured
Onward, flowing across the flowing wave.
Then on the waters fell
The shadow of man, and earth and the heavens scrawled
With names, as if each pebble and leaf would tell
The tale untellable.   And the Lord called
The seventh day forth and the glory of the Lord.

And now we see in the sun
The mountains standing clear in the third day
(Where they shall always stay)
And thence a river run,
Threading, clear cord of water, all to all:
The wooded hill and the cattle in the meadow,
The tall wave breaking on the high sea-wall,
The people at evening walking,
The crescent shadow
Of the light-built bridge, the hunter stalking
The flying quarry, each in a different morning,
The fish in the billow's heart, the man with the net,
The hungry swords crossed in the cross of warning,
The lion set
High on the banner, leaping into the sky,
The seasons playing
Their game of sun and moon and east and west,
The animal watching man and bird go by,
The women praying
For the passing of this fragmentary day
Into the day where all are gathered together,
Things and their names, in the storm's and the lightning's nest,
The seventh great day and the clear eternal weather.

ADAM'S DREAM

They say the first dream Adam our father had
After his agelong daydream in the Garden
When heaven and sun woke in his wakening mind,
The earth with all its hills and woods and waters,
The friendly tribes of trees and animals,
And earth's last wonder Eve (the first great dream
Which is the ground of every dream since then)—
They say he dreamt lying on the naked ground,
The gates shut fast behind him as he lay
Fallen in Eve's fallen arms, his terror drowned
In her engulfing terror, in the abyss
Whence there's no further fall, and comfort is—
That he was standing on a rocky ledge
High on a mountainside, bare crag behind,
In front a plain as far as eye could reach,
And on the plain a few small figures running
That were like men and women, yet were so far away
He could not see their faces. On they ran,
And fell, and rose again, and ran, and fell,
And rising were the same yet not the same,
Identical or interchangeable,
Different in indifference. As he looked
Still there were more of them, the plain was filling
As by an alien arithmetical magic
Unknown in Eden, a mechanical
Addition without meaning, joining only
Number to number in no mode or order,
Weaving no pattern. For these creatures moved
Towards no fixed mark even when in growing bands
They clashed against each other and clashing fell
In mounds of bodies. For they rose again,
Identical or interchangeable,

And went their way that was not like a way;
Some back and forward, back and forward, some
In a closed circle, wide or narrow, others
In zigzags on the sand. Yet all were busy,
And tense with purpose as they cut the air
Which seemed to press them back. Sometimes they paused
While one stopped one—fortuitous assignations
In the disorder, whereafter two by two
They ran awhile,
Then parted and again were single. Some
Ran straight against the frontier of the plain
Till the horizon drove them back. A few
Stood still and never moved. Then Adam cried
Out of his dream, 'What are you doing there?'
And the crag answered 'Are you doing there?'
'What are you doing there?'—'you doing there?'
The animals had withdrawn and from the caves
And woods stared out in fear or condemnation,
Like outlaws or like judges. All at once
Dreaming or half-remembering, 'This is time',
Thought Adam in his dream, and time was strange
To one lately in Eden. 'I must see',
He cried, 'the faces. Where are the faces? Who
Are you all out there?' Then in his changing dream
He was a little nearer, and he saw
They were about some business strange to him
That had a form and sequence past their knowledge ;
And that was why they ran so frenziedly.
Yet all, it seemed, made up a story, illustrated
By these the living, the unknowing, cast
Each singly for his part. But Adam longed
For more, not this mere moving pattern, not
This illustrated storybook of mankind
Always a-making, improvised on nothing.

At that he was among them, and saw each face
Was like his face, so that he would have hailed them
As sons of God but that something restrained him.
And he remembered all, Eden, the Fall,
The Promise, and his place, and took their hands
That were his hands, his and his children's hands,
Cried out and was at peace, and turned again
In love and grief in Eve's encircling arms.

OUTSIDE EDEN

A few lead in their harvest still
By the ruined wall and broken gate.
Far inland shines the radiant hill.
Inviolable the empty gate,
Impassable the gaping wall;
And the mountain over all.

Such is the country of this clan,
Haunted by guilt and innocence.
There is a sweetness in the air
That bloomed as soon as time began,
But now is dying everywhere.
This people guard in reverence
Their proud and famous family tree
Sprung from a glorious king who once
Lived in such boundless liberty
As never a one among the great
Has known in all the kingdoms since;
For death was barred from his estate.
Lost long ago, the histories say,
He and his consort lost it all.
Guiltiest and least guilty, they
In innocence discovered sin
Round a lost corner of the day,
And fell and fell through all the fall
That hurled them headlong over the wall.
Their children live where then they lay.

Guilt is next door to innocence.
So here this people choose to live
And never think to travel hence,
Nor learn to be inquisitive,

Nor browse in sin's great library,
The single never-ending book
That fills the shelves of all the earth.
There the learned enquirers look
And blind themselves to see their face.
But these live in the land of birth
And count all else an idle grace.

The simple have long memories.
Memory makes simple all that is.
So these the lawless world can love
At ease, the thickets running wild,
The thorny waste, the flourishing grove.
Their knotted landscape, wrong and clear
As the crude drawings of a child,
Is to them become more dear
Than geometrical symmetry.
Their griefs are all in memory grown
As natural as a weathered stone.
Their troubles are a tribute given
Freely while gazing at the hill.
Such is their simplicity,
Standing on earth, looking at heaven.

PROMETHEUS

The careless seasons pass and leave me here.
The forests rise like ghosts and fade like dreams.
All has its term; flowers flicker on the ground
A summer moment, and the rock is bare.
Alone the animals trace their changeless figure,
Embodying change. Agelong I watch the leopard
Glaring at something past the end of time,
And the wild goat immobile on his rock,
Lost in a trance of roaming through the skies:
I look and he is there. But pilgrim man
Travels foreknowing to his stopping place,
Awareness on his lips, which have tasted sorrow,
Foretasted death. These strangers do not know
Their happiness is in that which leads their sorrow
Round to an end. My hope is not like theirs.
I pray for the end of all things and this pain
Which makes me cry: Move faster, sun and stars,
And bear these chains and bear this body away
Into your flying circuit; freedom waits
There in the blessed nothingness that follows
The charging onset of the centaur-stars,
Trampling time out. For when these clamorous races
Lie silent in the ground from which they came,
And all the earth is quiet, a hush may fall
Even in the house of heaven, and the heedless gods
May raise their eyes to look and bid me come
Again among them, then when the feud is over
And fire and those in whom it blazed and died
Are strewn in ashes on the ashen hills.

What shall I say to the gods? Heaven will be strange,
And strange those scars inscribed in distant time.

Who will give answer to the earth's dark story?
Zeus with the ponderous glory of the bull,
Or the boy Eros with his fretful quiver?
What expectation there except at most
That this my knowledge will be an aeon's gossip?

The shrines are emptying and the peoples changing.
It may be I should find Olympus vacant
If I should return. For I have heard a wonder:
Lands without gods; nothing but earth and water;
Words without mystery; and the only creed
An iron text to beat the round skulls flat
And fit them for the cap of a buried master.
Strange ritual. Now time's storm is rising, sweeping
The sons of man into an emptier room,
Vast as a continent, bare as a desert,
Where the dust takes man's lifetime to revolve
Around the walls, harried by peevish gusts
And little spiteful eddies; nothing standing
But the cast-iron cities and rubbish mountains.

At the world's end to whom shall I tell the story?
A god came down, they say, from another heaven
Not in rebellion but in pity and love,
Was born a son of woman, lived and died,
And rose again with all the spoils of time
Back to his home, where now they are transmuted
Into bright toys and various frames of glory;
And time itself is there a world of marvels.
If I could find that god, he would hear and answer.

THE GRAVE OF PROMETHEUS

No one comes here now, neither god nor man.
For long the animals have kept away,
Scared by immortal cries and the scream of vultures;
Now by this silence. The heavenly thief who stole
Heaven's dangerous treasure turned to common earth
When that great company forsook Olympus.
The fire was out, and he became his barrow.
Ten yards long there he lay outstretched, and grass
Grew over him: all else in a breath forgotten.
Yet there you still may see a tongue of stone,
Shaped like a calloused hand where no hand should be,
Extended from the sward as if for alms,
Its palm all licked and blackened as with fire.
A mineral change made cool his fiery bed,
And made his burning body a quiet mound,
And his great face a vacant ring of daisies.

ORPHEUS' DREAM

And she was there. The little boat,
Coasting the perilous isles of sleep,
Zones of oblivion and despair,
Stopped, for Eurydice was there.
The foundering skiff could scarcely keep
All that felicity afloat.

As if we had left earth's frontier wood
Long since and from this sea had won
The lost original of the soul,
The moment gave us pure and whole
Each back to each, and swept us on
Past every choice to boundless good.

Forgiveness, truth, atonement, all
Our love at once—till we could dare
At last to turn our heads and see
The poor ghost of Eurydice
Still sitting in her silver chair,
Alone in Hades' empty hall.

THE OTHER OEDIPUS

Remembered on the Peloponnesian roads,
He and his serving-boy and his concubine,
White-headed and light-hearted, their true wits gone
Past the last stroke of time into a day
Without a yesterday or a to-morrow,
A brightness laid like a blue lake around them,
Or endless field to play or linger in.
They were so gay and innocent, you'd have thought
A god had won a glorious prize for them
In some celestial field, and the odds were gone,
Fate sent on holiday, the earth and heaven
Thenceforth in endless friendly talk together.
They were quite storyless and had clean forgotten
That memory burning in another world;
But they too leaf-light now for any story.
If anyone spoke a word of other guilt
By chance before them, then they stamped their feet
In rage and gnashed their teeth like peevish children.
But then forgot. The road their welcoming home.
They would not stay in a house or let a door
Be locked on them. The surly Spartan farmers
Were kind to them, pitying their happiness.

THE CHARM

There was a drug that Helen knew.
Dropped in the wine-cup it could take
All memory and all grief away,
And while the drinker, wide awake,
Sat in his chair, indifference grew
Around him in the estranging day.
He saw the colours shine and flow,
The giant lineaments break and change,
But all storyless, all strange.
The crystal spheres on Helen's brow
Took and gave back the coloured world,
Yet only seemed to smile or glare
At nothing but the empty air.
The serving women crossed the floor,
Swept by a silent tempest, whirled
Into the light and through the door.
This he saw and nothing more,
While all the charities, unborn,
Slept soundly in his burdened breast
As he took his heavy rest,
Careless, thoughtless and forlorn.

So strong the enchantment, Homer says,
That if this man's own son had died,
Killed at his feet, his dreaming gaze
(Like a false-hearted summer day
Watching the hunter and his prey
At ease) would not have changed at all,
Nor his heart knocked against his side.
But far within him something cried
For the great tragedy to start,
The pang in lingering mercy fall,
And sorrow break upon his heart.

TELEMACHOS REMEMBERS

Twenty years, every day,
The figures in the web she wove
Came and stood and went away.
Her fingers in their pitiless play
Beat downward as the shuttle drove.

Slowly, slowly did they come,
With horse and chariot, spear and bow,
Half-finished heroes sad and mum,
Came slowly to the shuttle's hum.
Time itself was not so slow.

And what at last was there to see?
A horse's head, a trunkless man,
Mere odds and ends about to be,
And the thin line of augury
Where through the web the shuttle ran.

How could she bear the mounting load,
Dare once again her ghosts to rouse?
Far away Odysseus trod
The treadmill of the turning road
That did not bring him to his house.

The weary loom, the weary loom,
The task grown sick from morn to night,
From year to year. The treadle's boom
Made a low thunder in the room.
The woven phantoms mazed her sight.

If she had pushed it to the end,
Followed the shuttle's cunning song

So far she had no thought to rend
In time the web from end to end,
She would have worked a matchless wrong.

Instead, that jumble of heads and spears,
Forlorn scraps of her treasure trove.
I wet them with my childish tears
Not knowing she wove into her fears
Pride and fidelity and love.

THE HEROES

When these in all their bravery took the knock
And like obedient children swaddled and bound
Were borne to sleep within the chambered rock,
A splendour broke from that impervious ground,
Which they would never know. Whence came that greatness?
No fiery chariot whirled them heavenwards, they
Saw no Elysium opening, but the straitness
Of full submission bound them where they lay.

What could that greatness be? It was not fame.
Yet now they seemed to grow as they grew less,
And where they lay were more than where they had stood.
They did not go to any beatitude.
They were stripped clean of feature, presence, name,
When that strange glory broke from namelessness.

ABRAHAM

The rivulet-loving wanderer Abraham
Through waterless wastes tracing his fields of pasture
Led his Chaldean herds and fattening flocks
With the meandering art of wavering water
That seeks and finds, yet does not know its way.
He came, rested and prospered, and went on,
Scattering behind him little pastoral kingdoms,
And over each one its own particular sky,
Not the great rounded sky through which he journeyed,
That went with him but when he rested changed.
His mind was full of names
Learned from strange peoples speaking alien tongues,
And all that was theirs one day he would inherit.
He died content and full of years, though still
The Promise had not come, and left his bones,
Far from his father's house, in alien Canaan.

THE SUCCESSION

Legendary Abraham,
The old Chaldean wanderer,
First among these peoples came,
Cruising above them like a star
That is in love with distances
And has through age to calmness grown,
Patient in the wilderness
And untarrying in the sown.
At last approached his setting mark.
Thence he sent his twin star out,
Isaac, to revolve alone.
For two great stars that through an age
Play in their corner of the sky,
Separate go into the dark,
And ere they end their roundabout
One must live and one must die.

Isaac in his tutelage
Wheeled around the father light.
Then began his pilgrimage
Through another day and night,
Other peoples, other lands.
Where the father could not go
There is gone the careless son.
He can never miss his way.
By strangers' hands to strangers' hands
He is carried where he will.
Free, he must the powers obey,
Serve, be served by good and ill,
Safe through all the hazards run.
All shall watch him come and go
Until his quittance he has won;
And Jacob wheels into the day.

We through the generations came
Here by a way we do not know
From the fields of Abraham,
And still the road is scarce begun.
To hazard and to danger go
The sallying generations all
Where the imperial highways run.
And our songs and legends call
The hazard and the danger good;
For our fathers understood
That danger was by hope begot
And hazard by revolving chance
Since first we drew the enormous lot.

THE ROAD

The great road stretched before them, clear and still,
Then from in front one cried: 'Turn back! Turn back!'
Yet they had never seen so fine a track,
Honest and frank past any thought of ill.
But when they glanced behind, how strange, how strange,
These wild demented windings in and out—
Traced by some devil of mischief or of doubt?—
That was the road they had come by. Could it change?

How could they penetrate that perilous maze
Backwards, again, climb backwards down the scree
From the wrong side, slither among the dead?
Yet as they travelled on, for many days
These words rang in their ears as if they said,
'There was another road you did not see.'

THE ANNUNCIATION

The angel and the girl are met.
Earth was the only meeting place.
For the embodied never yet
Travelled beyond the shore of space.
The eternal spirits in freedom go.

See, they have come together, see,
While the destroying minutes flow,
Each reflects the other's face
Till heaven in hers and earth in his
Shine steady there. He's come to her
From far beyond the farthest star,
Feathered through time. Immediacy
Of strangest strangeness is the bliss
That from their limbs all movement takes.
Yet the increasing rapture brings
So great a wonder that it makes
Each feather tremble on his wings.

Outside the window footsteps fall
Into the ordinary day
And with the sun along the wall
Pursue their unreturning way
That was ordained in eternity.
Sound's perpetual roundabout
Rolls its numbered octaves out
And hoarsely grinds its battered tune.

But through the endless afternoon
These neither speak nor movement make,
But stare into their deepening trance
As if their gaze would never break.

THE CHRISTMAS

Now Christmas comes. The menial earth
   Lays by its worn and sweaty gear
And strews with emblems of rebirth
   The burial of the solar year.

Midnight strikes. One star awake
   Watches the Mother and the Child
Who with his little hands will make
   Spring blossom in the winter wild.

This star that left the ordered throng
   Caused no confusion in the night,
Nor strayed to prove his brothers wrong,
   But told that all the stars were right.

Three little days with lengthening glow
   Sets the great year upon its way;
An infant's cry across the snow
   Rouses the never-setting day.

A Child, a God, he will respire
   Obediently time's mortal breath,
Freely work out his double hire,
   Endless enact a Birth, a Death,

Accomplishing the miracle,
   The marriage feast of heaven and earth,
Of which on earth we cannot tell
   Save in such words: a Death, a Birth.

The childish starlight glimmers near
   In the green firmament of the tree,
And the soft dreaming of the year
   Leads in Judaea and Galilee.

THE SON

This hungry flesh and bone
That white and black and brown
Share was shared by One
Once who to death went down.

Son of God and of Man,
He breathed as ours his breath,
And in this body ran
The crooked road to death.

Night and day and night
Wheeled him through time and space,
Whose hour was changeless light,
Infinity his place.

Time's essential heat
Bound him inside the womb
And in his arteries beat
The proud march to the tomb.

He from eternity
Stared now through a little eye,
That God and Man might see
The good and the wicked die.

Born, his babbling tongue
Told infancy's helplessness,
Disgrace of being young,
Adolescent distress,

Till manhood's brutal force
Through all his veins rolled on
Wild as a headstrong horse,
Though he was Heaven's son.

Thirst like a rusty knife,
Dry hunger he withstood,
Who had the water of life
And the immortal food.

The skill of the carpenter,
The sailor's dauntless heart
He learned, lest he should mar,
A God, his second part.

Happiness not of Heaven,
And unimmortal sorrows
He chose, talk in the evening,
And the wild mounting morrows

That wound in narrowing rings
Up to the waiting Tree
Through treachery of things
And men's treachery.

Till only despair was left;
'Me why hast Thou forsaken?'
God of God bereft
Down from the tree was taken,

That so the Light shine through
The first to the last pain,
And all be made new
Down to the last grain.

Ordinary men
Saw him take his fall.
All is changed since then;
He is joined with all.

THE KILLING

That was the day they killed the Son of God
On a squat hill-top by Jerusalem.
Zion was bare, her children from their maze
Sucked by the demon curiosity
Clean through the gates. The very halt and blind
Had somehow got themselves up to the hill.

After the ceremonial preparation,
The scourging, nailing, nailing against the wood,
Erection of the main-trees with their burden,
While from the hill rose an orchestral wailing,
They were there at last, high up in the soft spring day.
We watched the writhings, heard the moanings, saw
The three heads turning on their separate axles
Like broken wheels left spinning. Round *his* head
Was loosely bound a crown of plaited thorn
That hurt at random, stinging temple and brow
As the pain swung into its envious circle.
In front the wreath was gathered in a knot
That as he gazed looked like the last stump left
Of a death-wounded deer's great antlers. Some
Who came to stare grew silent as they looked,
Indignant or sorry. But the hardened old
And the hard-hearted young, although at odds
From the first morning, cursed him with one curse,
Having prayed for a Rabbi or an armed Messiah
And found the Son of God. What use to them
Was a God or a Son of God? Of what avail
For purposes such as theirs? Beside the cross-foot,
Alone, four women stood and did not move
All day. The sun revolved, the shadow wheeled,
The evening fell. His head lay on his breast,

But in his breast they watched his heart move on
By itself alone, accomplishing its journey.
Their taunts grew louder, sharpened by the knowledge
That he was walking in the park of death,
Far from their rage. Yet all grew stale at last,
Spite, curiosity, envy, hate itself.
They waited only for death and death was slow
And came so quietly they scarce could mark it.
They were angry then with death and death's deceit.

I was a stranger, could not read these people
Or this outlandish deity. Did a God
Indeed in dying cross my life that day
By chance, he on his road and I on mine?

LOST AND FOUND

That by which we have lost and still shall lose
Even what we win (but never fully win,)
It gave the choice without the skill to choose,
The rough-cast world, the broken Eden within,
Taught us the narrow miss and the accident,
The countless odds and the predestined plot,
Action and thought to every bias bent,
And chance, the winning and the losing lot.

It gave us time, and time gave us the story,
Beginning and end in one wild largesse spent,
Inexplicable. Until the heavenly Glory
Took on our flesh and wrought the meaning. Since,
Sons, daughters, brothers, sisters of that Prince
Are we, by grace, although in banishment.

ANTICHRIST

He walks, the enchanter, on his sea of glass,
Poring upon his blue inverted heaven
Where a false sun revolves from west to east.
If he could raise his eyes he would see his hell.
In him all is reversed; evil is good.
He is no spirit, nor a spirit's shadow,
But a mere toy shaped by ingenious devils
To bring discomfiture on credulous man.
He's the false copy where each feature's wrong,
Yet so disposed the whole gives a resemblance.
When he's in anguish smiles writhe on his lips
And will not stop. His imperturbable brow
Is carved by rage not his but theirs that made him,
For he's a nothing where they move in freedom,
Knowing that nothing's there. When he forgives
It is for love of sin not of the sinner.
He takes sin for his province, knows sin only,
Nothing but sin from end to end of the world.
He heals the sick to show his conjuring skill,
Vexed only by the cure; and turns his cheek
To goad the furious to more deadly fury,
And damn by a juggling trick the ingenuous sinner.
He brings men from the dead to tell the living
That their undoing is a common fetch.
Ingeniously he postures on the Tree
(His crowning jest), an actor miming death,
While his indifferent mind is idly pleased
That treason should run on through time for ever.
His vast indulgence is so free and ample,
You well might think it universal love,
For all seems goodness, sweetness, harmony.
He is the Lie; one true thought, and he's gone.

44

THE LORD

They could not tell me who should be my lord,
But I could read from every word they said
The common thought: Perhaps that lord was dead,
And only a story now and a wandering word.
How could I follow a word or serve a fable,
They asked me. 'Here are lords a-plenty. Take
Service with one, if only for your sake;
Yet better be your own master if you're able.'

I would rather scour the roads, a masterless dog,
Than take such service, be a public fool,
Obstreperous or tongue-tied, a good rogue,
Than be with those, the clever and the dull,
Who say that lord is dead; when I can hear
Daily his dying whisper in my ear.

ONE FOOT IN EDEN

One foot in Eden still, I stand
And look across the other land.
The world's great day is growing late,
Yet strange these fields that we have planted
So long with crops of love and hate.
Time's handiworks by time are haunted,
And nothing now can separate
The corn and tares compactly grown.
The armorial weed in stillness bound
About the stalk; these are our own.
Evil and good stand thick around
In the fields of charity and sin
Where we shall lead our harvest in.

Yet still from Eden springs the root
As clean as on the starting day.
Time takes the foliage and the fruit
And burns the archetypal leaf
To shapes of terror and of grief
Scattered along the winter way.
But famished field and blackened tree
Bear flowers in Eden never known.
Blossoms of grief and charity
Bloom in these darkened fields alone.
What had Eden ever to say
Of hope and faith and pity and love
Until was buried all its day
And memory found its treasure trove?
Strange blessings never in Paradise
Fall from these beclouded skies.

THE INCARNATE ONE

The windless northern surge, the sea-gull's scream,
And Calvin's kirk crowning the barren brae.
I think of Giotto the Tuscan shepherd's dream,
Christ, man and creature in their inner day.
How could our race betray
The Image, and the Incarnate One unmake
Who chose this form and fashion for our sake?

The Word made flesh here is made word again,
A word made word in flourish and arrogant crook.
See there King Calvin with his iron pen,
And God three angry letters in a book,
And there the logical hook
On which the Mystery is impaled and bent
Into an ideological instrument.

There's better gospel in man's natural tongue,
And truer sight was theirs outside the Law
Who saw the far side of the Cross among
The archaic peoples in their ancient awe,
In ignorant wonder saw
The wooden cross-tree on the bare hillside,
Not knowing that there a God suffered and died.

The fleshless word, growing, will bring us down,
Pagan and Christian man alike will fall,
The auguries say, the white and black and brown,
The merry and sad, theorist, lover, all
Invisibly will fall :
Abstract calamity, save for those who can
Build their cold empire on the abstract man.

A soft breeze stirs and all my thoughts are blown
Far out to sea and lost. Yet I know well
The bloodless word will battle for its own
Invisibly in brain and nerve and cell.
The generations tell
Their personal tale: the One has far to go
Past the mirages and the murdering snow.

SCOTLAND'S WINTER

Now the ice lays its smooth claws on the sill,
The sun looks from the hill
Helmed in his winter casket,
And sweeps his arctic sword across the sky.
The water at the mill
Sounds more hoarse and dull.
The miller's daughter walking by
With frozen fingers soldered to her basket
Seems to be knocking
Upon a hundred leagues of floor
With her light heels, and mocking
Percy and Douglas dead,
And Bruce on his burial bed,
Where he lies white as may
With wars and leprosy,
And all the kings before
This land was kingless,
And all the singers before
This land was songless,
This land that with its dead and living waits the Judgment Day.
But they, the powerless dead,
Listening can hear no more
Than a hard tapping on the sounding floor
A little overhead
Of common heels that do not know
Whence they come or where they go
And are content
With their poor frozen life and shallow banishment.

THE GREAT HOUSE

However it came, this great house has gone down
Unconquered into chaos (as you might see
A famous ship warped to a rotting quay
In miles of weeds and rubbish, once a town.)
So the great house confronts the brutish air,
And points its turrets towards the hidden sky,
While in the dark the flags of honour fly
Where faith and hope and bravery would not dare.

Accident did not do this, nor mischance.
But so must order to disorder come
At their due time, and honour take its stance
Deep in dishonour's ground. Chaos is new,
And has no past or future. Praise the few
Who built in chaos our bastion and our home.

THE EMBLEM

I who so carefully keep in such repair
The six-inch king and the toy treasury,
Prince, poet, realm shrivelled in time's black air,
I am not, although I seem, an antiquary.
For that scant-acre kingdom is not dead,
Nor save in seeming shrunk. When at its gate,
Which you pass daily, you incline your head,
And enter (do not knock; it keeps no state)

You will be with space and order magistral,
And that contracted world so vast will grow
That this will seem a little tangled field.
For you will be in very truth with all
In their due place and honour, row on row.
For this I read the emblem on the shield.

II

TO FRANZ KAFKA

If we, the proximate damned, presumptive blest,
Were called one day to some high consultation
With the authentic ones, the worst and best
Picked from all time, how mean would be our station.
Oh we could never bear the standing shame,
Equivocal ignominy of non-election;
We who will hardly answer to our name,
And on the road direct ignore direction.

But you, dear Franz, sad champion of the drab
And half, would watch the tell-tale shames drift in
(As if they were troves of treasure) not aloof,
But with a famishing passion quick to grab
Meaning, and read on all the leaves of sin
Eternity's secret script, the saving proof.

EFFIGIES

1

His glances were directive, seemed to move
Pawns on a secret chess-board. You could fancy
You saw the pieces in their wooden dance
Pass in geometrical obedience
From square to square, or stop like broken clockwork
When silence spoke its checkmate. Past that arena
Stretched out a winding moonlight labyrinth,
A shining limbo filled with vanishing faces,
Propitious or dangerous, to be scanned
In a passion of repulsion or desire.
His glances knew two syllables: 'Come' and 'Go'.
When he was old and dull his eyes grew weary,
Gazing so long into the shifting maze,
And narrowed to the semi-circle before him,
The last defence. There if a stranger entered,
His heart, that beat regardless far within,
Grew still, a hawk before the deadly drop,
Then beat again as his quick mind found the gambit.
All this he hardly knew. His face was like
The shining front of a rich and loveless house,
The doors all shut. The windows cast such brightness
Outwards that none could see what was within,
Half-blinded by the strong repelling dazzle.
Set in the doors two little judas windows
Sometimes would catch the timid visitor's eye
And he would grow aware of a nameless something,
Animal or human, watching his approach,
Like darkness out of darkness. When he was dying
The pieces sauntered freely about the board
Like lawless vagrants, and would not be controlled.

He would whisper 'Stop,'
Starting awake, and weep to think they were free.

2

Pity the poor betrayer in the maze
That closed about him when he set the trap
To catch his friend. Now he is there alone,
The envied and beloved quarry fled
Long since for death and freedom. And the maze
Is like an odd device to marvel at
With other eyes if other eyes could see it;
As curious as an idle prince's toy.
There he is now, lost in security,
Quite, quite inside, no fissure in the walls,
Nor any sign of the door that let him in;
Only the oblivious labyrinth all around.
He did not dream of the trap within the trap
In the mad moment, nor that he would long
Sometime to have the beloved victim there
For the deep winding dialogue without end.
Pity him, for he cannot think the thought
Nor feel the pang that yet might set him free,
And Judas ransomed dangle from the tree.

3

Revolving in his own
Immovable danger zone,
Having killed his enemy
And betrayed his troublesome friend
To be with himself alone,
He watched upon the floor
The punctual minutes crawl

Towards the remaining wall
That opened in eternity,
And thought, 'Here is the end.'
Cut off in blind desire,
From the window he would see,
Twisting in twisted glass,
The devastated street,
The houses all gone wrong,
Watch hats and hurrying feet,
Wild birds and horses pass,
Think, 'All shall go up in fire,
Horse, man and city, all.'
Or dream a whole day long
Of miles and miles of way
Through hills down to the sea
At peace in a distant day;
Gazing upon the floor.
No knock upon the door.

4

We fired and fired, and yet they would not fall,
But stood on the ridge and bled,
Transfixed against the sky as on a wall,
Though they and we knew they were dead.
Then we went on,
Passed through them or between;
But all our eyes could fasten upon
Was a great broken machine,
Or so it seemed. Then on the ridge ahead
We watched them rise again.
I do not think we knew the dead
Were real, or really dead, till then.

She lived in comfort on her poor few pence
And sweetly starved to feed her swelling dream
Where all she had done came back in grievous blessing.
She had left her house and was by her lover left,
Her flying wings struck root upon his shoulders,
And in the self-same flight bore him away.
Her life was all an aria and an echo,
And when the aria ceased the echo led her
Gently to alight somewhere that seemed the earth.
There gradually she withered towards her harvest,
That grew as she grew less, until at last
She stared in grief at mounds and mounds of grain.

THE DIFFICULT LAND

This is a difficult land. Here things miscarry
Whether we care, or do not care enough.
The grain may pine, the harlot weed grow haughty,
Sun, rain, and frost alike conspire against us:
You'd think there was malice in the very air.
And the spring floods and summer droughts: our fields
Mile after mile of soft and useless dust.
On dull delusive days presaging rain
We yoke the oxen, go out harrowing,
Walk in the middle of an ochre cloud,
Dust rising before us and falling again behind us,
Slowly and gently settling where it lay.
These days the earth itself looks sad and senseless.
And when next day the sun mounts hot and lusty
We shake our fists and kick the ground in anger.
We have strange dreams: as that, in the early morning
We stand and watch the silver drift of stars
Turn suddenly to a flock of black-birds flying.
And once in a lifetime men from over the border,
In early summer, the season of fresh campaigns,
Come trampling down the corn, and kill our cattle.
These things we know and by good luck or guidance
Either frustrate or, if we must, endure.
We are a people; race and speech support us,
Ancestral rite and custom, roof and tree,
Our songs that tell of our triumphs and disasters
(Fleeting alike), continuance of fold and hearth,
Our names and callings, work and rest and sleep,
And something that, defeated, still endures—
These things sustain us. Yet there are times
When name, identity, and our very hands,
Senselessly labouring, grow most hateful to us,

And we would gladly rid us of these burdens
(Which yet are knit to us as flesh to bone),
Enter our darkness through the doors of wheat
And the light veil of grass (leaving behind
Name, body, country, speech, vocation, faith)
And gather into the secrecy of the earth
Furrowed by broken ploughs lost deep in time.

We have such hours, but are drawn back again
By faces of goodness, faithful masks of sorrow,
Honesty, kindness, courage, fidelity,
The love that lasts a life's time. And the fields,
Homestead and stall and barn, springtime and autumn.
(For we can love even the wandering seasons
In their inhuman circuit.) And the dead
Who lodge in us so strangely, unremembered,
Yet in their place. For how can we reject
The long last look on the ever-dying face
Turned backward from the other side of time?
And how offend the dead and shame the living
By these despairs? And how refrain from love?
This is a difficult country, and our home.

NOTHING THERE BUT FAITH

Nothing, it seemed, between them and the grave.
No, as I looked, there was nothing anywhere.
You'd think no ground could be so flat and bare:
No little ridge or hump or bush to brave
The horizon. Yet they called that land their land,
Without a single thought drank in that air
As simple and equivocal as despair.
This, this was what I could not understand.

The reason was, there was nothing there but faith.
Faith made the whole, yes all they could see or hear
Or touch or think, and arched its break of day
Within them and around them every way.
They looked: all was transfigured far and near,
And the great world rolled between them and death.

DOUBLE ABSENCE

The rust-red moon above the rose-red cloud,
Ethereal gifts of the absconding sun
That now is shining full on other lands
And soon will draw its track a hundred miles
Across the quiet breast of the hushed Atlantic.
The smoke grows up, solid, an ashen tree
From the high Abbey chimney. A sycamore
Holds on its topmost tip a singing thrush,
Its breast turned towards the sign of the buried sun.
Chance only brings such rare felicities
Beyond contrivance of the adventuring mind,
Strange past all meaning, set in their place alone.
Now the moon rises clear and fever pale
Out from the cloud's dissolving drift of ashes,
While in my mind, in double absence, hangs
The rust-red moon above the rose-red cloud.

DAY AND NIGHT

I wrap the blanket of the night
About me, fold on fold on fold—
And remember how as a child
Lost in the newness of the light
I first discovered what is old
From the night and the soft night wind.
For in the daytime all was new,
Moving in light and in the mind
All at once, thought, shape and hue.
Extravagant novelty too wild
For the new eyes of a child.

The night, the night alone is old
And showed me only what I knew,
Knew, yet never had been told;
A speech that from the darkness grew
Too deep for daily tongues to say,
Archaic dialogue of a few
Upon the sixth or the seventh day.
And shapes too simple for a place
In the day's shrill complexity
Came and were more natural, more
Expected than my father's face
Smiling across the open door,
More simple than the sanded floor
In unexplained simplicity.

A man now, gone with time so long—
My youth to myself grown fabulous
Like an old land's memories, a song
To trouble or to pleasure us—
I try to fit that world to this,

The hidden to the visible play,
Would have them both, would nothing miss,
Learn from the shepherd of the dark,
Here in the light, the paths to know
That thread the labyrinthine park,
And the great Roman roads that go
Striding across the untrodden day.

THE OTHER STORY

How for the new thing can there be a word?
How can we know
The act, the form itself, unnamed, unheard,
Or for the first time go
Again on the road that runs ere memory
Snares it in syllables
And rings its burial bells
In gossip or music or poetry?
Yet we would not remember, but would be.

Why should we muse
On this great world that always is no more,
Or hope to hear sometime the great lost news?
It was all before.
And we would be where we were bred,
In Eden an hour away,
Though still our cheeks are red
For what is only in remembrance
Revolt or sin or guilt or shame,
Or some word much the same,
But was a haze of blood from foot to head,
Was that, and nothing said.
Innocent, knowing nothing of innocence,
We learned it from the sad memorial name
First uttered by the offence.
And now the two words seem
A single, fabulous, reciprocal glory,
A dream re-enacted in another dream,
And all accomplished as we plucked the bough.

Stories we know. There is another story.
If one of you is innocent let him tell it now.

DREAM AND THING

This is the thing, this truly is the thing.
We dreamt it once; now it has come about.
That was the dream, but this, this is the thing.
The dream was bold and thought it could foretell
What time would bring, but time, it seems, can bring
Only this thing which never has had a doubt
That everything is much like everything,
And the deep family likeness will come out.
We thought the dream would spread its folded wing;
But here's a thing that's neither sick nor well,
Stupid nor wise, and has no story to tell,
Though every tale is about it and about.
That is the thing, that is the very thing.
Yet take another look and you may bring
From the dull mass each separate splendour out.
There is no trust but in the miracle.

SONG FOR A HYPOTHETICAL AGE

Grief, they have said, is personal,
Else there'd be no grief at all.
We, exempt from grief and rage,
Rule here our new impersonal age.
Now while dry is every eye
The last grief is passing by.
History takes its final turn
Where all's to mourn for, none to mourn.
Idle justice sits alone
In a world to order grown.
Justice never shed a tear,
And if justice we would bear
We must get another face,
Find a smoother tale to tell
Where everything is in its place
And happiness inevitable.

(Long, long ago, the old men say,
A famous wife, Penelope,
For twenty years the pride of Greece,
Wove and unwove a web all day
That might have been a masterpiece—
If she had let it have its way—
To drive all artistry to despair
And set the sober world at play
Beyond the other side of care,
And lead a fabulous era in.
But still she said, 'Where I begin
Must I return, else all is lost,
And great Odysseus tempest-tossed
Will perish, shipwrecked on my art.
But so, I guide him to the shore.'

And again the web she tore,
No more divided from her heart.)

Oh here the hot heart petrifies
And the round earth to rock is grown
In the winter of our eyes;
Heart and earth a single stone.
Until the stony barrier break
Grief and joy no more shall wake.

THE YOUNG PRINCES

There was a time: we were young princelings then
In artless state, with brows as bright and clear
As morning light on a new morning land.
We gave and took with innocent hands, not knowing
If we were rich or poor, or thinking at all
Of yours or mine; we were newcomers still,
And to have asked the use of that or this,
Its price, commodity, profit would have been
Discourtesy to it and shame to us.
We saw the earth stretched out to us in welcome,
But in our hearts we were the welcomers,
And so were courteous to all that was
In high simplicity and natural pride
To be so hailed and greeted with such glory
(Like absentminded kings who are proffered all
And need not have a penny in their pockets).
And when the elders told the ancestral stories,
Even as they spoke we knew the characters,
The good and bad, the simple and sly, the heroes,
Each in his place, and chance that turns the tale
To grief or joy; we saw and accepted all.
Then in the irreversible noonday came,
Showering its darts into our open breasts,
Doubt that kills courtesy and gratitude.
Since then we have led our dull discourteous lives,
Heaven doubting and earth doubting. Earth and heaven
Bent to our menial use. And yet sometimes
We still, as through a dream that comes and goes,
Know what we are, remembering what we were.

THE CLOUD

One late spring evening in Bohemia,
Driving to the Writers' House, we lost our way
In a maze of little winding roads that led
To nothing but themselves,
Weaving a rustic web for thoughtless travellers.
No house was near, nor sign or sound of life:
Only a chequer-board of little fields,
Crumpled and dry, neat squares of powdered dust.
At a sudden turn we saw
A young man harrowing, hidden in dust; he seemed
A prisoner walking in a moving cloud
Made by himself for his own purposes;
And there he grew and was as if exalted
To more than man, yet not, not glorified:
A pillar of dust moving in dust; no more.
The bushes by the roadside were encrusted
With a hard sheath of dust.
We looked and wondered; the dry cloud moved on
With its interior image.
                                    Presently we found
A road that brought us to the Writers' House,
And there a preacher from Urania
(Sad land where hope each day is killed by hope)
Praised the good dust, man's ultimate salvation,
And cried that God was dead. As we drove back
Late to the city, still our minds were teased
By the brown barren fields, the harrowing,
The figure walking in its cloud, the message
From far Urania. This was before the change;
And in our memory cloud and message fused,
Image and thought condensed to a giant form
That walked the earth clothed in its earthly cloud,

Dust made sublime in dust. And yet it seemed unreal
And lonely as things not in their proper place.
And thinking of the man
Hid in his cloud we longed for light to break
And show that his face was the face once broken in Eden,
Beloved, world-without-end lamented face;
And not a blindfold mask on a pillar of dust.

THE HORSES

Barely a twelvemonth after
The seven days war that put the world to sleep,
Late in the evening the strange horses came.
By then we had made our covenant with silence,
But in the first few days it was so still
We listened to our breathing and were afraid.
On the second day
The radios failed; we turned the knobs; no answer.
On the third day a warship passed us, heading north,
Dead bodies piled on the deck. On the sixth day
A plane plunged over us into the sea. Thereafter
Nothing. The radios dumb;
And still they stand in corners of our kitchens,
And stand, perhaps, turned on, in a million rooms
All over the world. But now if they should speak,
If on a sudden they should speak again,
If on the stroke of noon a voice should speak,
We would not listen, we would not let it bring
That old bad world that swallowed its children quick
At one great gulp. We would not have it again.
Sometimes we think of the nations lying asleep,
Curled blindly in impenetrable sorrow,
And then the thought confounds us with its strangeness.

The tractors lie about our fields; at evening
They look like dank sea-monsters couched and waiting.
We leave them where they are and let them rust:
'They'll moulder away and be like other loam'.
We make our oxen drag our rusty ploughs,
Long laid aside. We have gone back
Far past our fathers' land.
                              And then, that evening
Late in the summer the strange horses came.

We heard a distant tapping on the road,
A deepening drumming; it stopped, went on again
And at the corner changed to hollow thunder.
We saw the heads
Like a wild wave charging and were afraid.
We had sold our horses in our fathers' time
To buy new tractors. Now they were strange to us
As fabulous steeds set on an ancient shield
Or illustrations in a book of knights.
We did not dare go near them. Yet they waited,
Stubborn and shy, as if they had been sent
By an old command to find our whereabouts
And that long-lost archaic companionship.
In the first moment we had never a thought
That they were creatures to be owned and used.
Among them were some half-a-dozen colts
Dropped in some wilderness of the broken world,
Yet new as if they had come from their own Eden.
Since then they have pulled our ploughs and borne our loads,
But that free servitude still can pierce our hearts.
Our life is changed; their coming our beginning.

SONG

This will not pass so soon,
Dear friend, this will not pass,
Though time is out of tune
With all beneath the moon,
Man and woman and flower and grass.
These will not pass.
For there's a word 'Return'
That's known among the quick and the dead,
Making two realms for ever cry and mourn.
So mourns the land of darkness when
Into the light away the lily is led,
And so gives thanks again
When from the earth the snow-pale beauty goes
Back to her home. Persephone,
Surely all this can only be
A light exchange and amorous interplay
In your strange twofold immortality;
And a diversion for a summer day
The death and resurrection of the rose.

THE ISLAND

Your arms will clasp the gathered grain
For your good time, and wield the flail
In merry fire and summer hail.
There stand the golden hills of corn
Which all the heroic clans have borne,
And bear the herdsmen of the plain,
The horseman in the mountain pass,
The archaic goat with silver horn,
Man, dog and flock and fruitful hearth,
And dynasties stretched beneath the grass.
Harvests of men to men give birth.
These the ancestral faces bred
And show as through a golden glass
Dances and temples of the dead.
Here speak through the transmuted tongue
The full grape bursting in the press,
The barley seething in the vat,
Which earth and man as one confess,
Babbling of what both would be at
In winding story and drunken song.
Though come a different destiny,
Though fall a universal wrong
More stern than simple savagery,
Men are made of what is made,
The meat, the drink, the life, the corn,
Laid up by them, in them reborn.
And self-begotten cycles close
About our way; indigenous art
And simple spells make unafraid
The haunted labyrinths of the heart,
And with our wild succession braid
The resurrection of the rose.

Sicily

76

INTO THIRTY CENTURIES BORN

Into thirty centuries born,
At home in them all but the very last,
We meet ourselves at every turn
In the long country of the past.
There the fallen are up again
In mortality's second day,
There the indisputable dead
Rise in flesh more fine than clay
And the dead selves we cast away
In imperfection are perfected,
And all is plain yet never found out!
Ilium burns before our eyes
For thirty centuries never put out,
And we walk the streets of Troy
And breathe in the air its fabulous name.
The king, the courtier and the rout
Shall never perish in that flame;
Old Priam shall become a boy
For ever changed, for ever the same.
What various sights these countries show:
The horses on the roundabout
Still flying round the glittering ring
That rusted fifty years ago.
The gunboat in the little bay,
A mile, and half an age away.
Methuselah letting the years go by
While death was new and still in doubt
And only a dream the thought, 'To die'.
And round a corner you may see
Man, maid and tempter under the tree:
You'd think there was no sense in death.
And nothing to remedy, nothing to blame;

The dark Enchanter is your friend.
Is it fantasy or faith
That keeps intact that marvellous show
And saves the helpless dead from harm?—
To-morrow sounds the great alarm
That puts the histories to rout;
To-morrow and to-morrow brings
Endless beginning without end.

Then on this moment set your foot,
Take your road for everywhere,
And from your roving barrier shoot
Your arrow into the empty air.
Follow at a careful pace,
Else you may wander in despair.
Gathered at your moving post
Is all that you have but memory.
This is the place of hope and fear,
And faith that comes when hope is lost.
Defeat and victory both are here.
In this place where all's to be,
In this moment you are free,
And bound to all. For you shall know
Before you Troy goes up in fire,
And you shall walk the Trojan streets
When home are sailed the murdering fleets,
Priam shall be a little boy,
Time shall cancel time's deceits,
And you shall weep for grief and joy
To see the whole world perishing
Into everlasting spring,
And over and over the opening briar.

MY OWN

There's nothing here to keep me from my own.—
The confident roads that at their ease beguile me
With the all-promising lands, the great unknown,
Can with their gilded dust blind me, defile me.
It's so. Yet never did their lies deceive me,
And when, lost in the dreaming route, I say
I seek my soul, my soul does not believe me,
But from these transports turns displeased away.

But then, but then, why should I so behave me,
Willingly duped ten, twenty times an hour,
But that even at my dearest cost I'd save me
From the true knowledge and the real power?
In which through all time's changeable seasons grown,
I might have stayed, unshaken, with my own.

THE CHOICE

The prisoner wasting in the pit,
The player bending over the strings,
The wise man tangled in his wit,
The angel grafted to his wings
Are governed by necessity,
Condemned to be whatever they are
Nor once from that to move away,
Each his appointed prisoner.
But the riddling sages say,
It is your prison that sets you free,
Else chaos would appropriate all.
Out of chaos you built this wall,
Raised this hovel of bone and clay
To be a refuge for liberty.

IF I COULD KNOW

If I could truly know that I do know
This, and the foreshower of this show,
Who is myself, for plot and scene are mine,
They say, and the world my sign,
Man, earth and heaven, co-patterned so or so—
If I could know.

If I could swear that I do truly see
The real world, and all itself and free,
Not prisoned in my shallow sight's confine,
Nor mine, but to be mine,
Freely sometime to come and be with me—
If I could see.

If I could tell that I do truly hear
A music, not this tumult in my ear
Of all that cries in the world, confused or fine;
If there were staff and sign
Pitched high above the battle of hope and fear—
If I could hear.

Make me to see and hear that I may know
This journey and the place towards which I go;
For a beginning and an end are mine
Surely, and have their sign
Which I and all in the earth and the heavens show.
Teach me to know.

THE LATE WASP

You that through all the dying summer
Came every morning to our breakfast table,
A lonely bachelor mummer,
And fed on the marmalade
So deeply, all your strength was scarcely able
To prise you from the sweet pit you had made,—
You and the earth have now grown older,
And your blue thoroughfares have felt a change;
They have grown colder;
And it is strange
How the familiar avenues of the air
Crumble now, crumble; the good air will not hold,
All cracked and perished with the cold;
And down you dive through nothing and through despair.

THE LATE SWALLOW

Leave, leave your well-loved nest,
Late swallow, and fly away.
Here is no rest
For hollowing heart and wearying wing.
Your comrades all have flown
To seek their southern paradise
Across the great earth's downward sloping side,
And you are alone.
Why should you cling
Still to the swiftly ageing narrowing day?
Prepare;
Shake out your pinions long untried
That now must bear you there where you would be
Through all the heavens of ice;
Till falling down the homing air
You light and perch upon the radiant tree.

SONG

This that I give and take,
This that I keep and break,
Is and is not my own
But lives in itself alone,
Yet is between us two,
Mine only in the breaking,
It all in the remaking,
Doing what I undo.

With it all must be well,
There where the invisible
Loom sweetly plies its trade.
All made there is well-made.
So be it between us two;
A giving be our taking,
A making our unmaking,
A doing what we undo.